SPORT IN 30 SECONDS

First published in the UK in 2019 by

Ivy Kids

An imprint of The Quarto Group

The Old Brewery

6 Blundell Street

London N7 9BH

United Kingdom

www.QuartoKnows.com

British Library Cataloguing-in-Publication Data
A catalogue record for this book is available from the British Library.

ISBN: 978-1-78240-622-8

This book was conceived, designed & produced by

Ivy Kids

58 West Street, Brighton, BN1 2RA, United Kingdom

PUBLISHER	Susan Kelly
CREATIVE DIRECTOR	Michael Whitehead
COMMISSIONING EDITOR	Susie Behar
PROJECT EDITOR	Hazel Songhurst
ART DIRECTOR	Hanri van Wyk
IN-HOUSE DESIGNER	Kate Haynes
DESIGNER	Suzie Harrison
ASSISTANT EDITOR	Lucy Menzies

Printed in China

10 9 8 7 6 5 4 3 2 1

SPORT
IN 30 SECONDS

PROF. JOHN BREWER

ILLUSTRATED BY TOM WOOLLEY
CONSULTANT: DR. JESSICA HILL

IVY KIDS

Contents

About this book
. . . in 60 seconds

Sport is exciting, challenging and fun! Millions of people all over the world enjoy playing and watching it.

But taking part in sport isn't just about winning medals or competing in World and Olympic Championships. We enjoy it too, and science has shown that exercise helps to make the human body fitter and healthier.

Have you ever wondered how sports first began and who the first competitors were? Evidence tells us that wrestling contests were part of life in prehistoric societies. And that over 2,000 years ago, at the first Olympic Games, the winning athletes were seen as heroes – just as they are today.

Sport didn't become truly global until the 20th century. For hundreds of years, sports and games were usually played in local communities. Rules were often made up and fighting was common! By the 1800s, ideas about the value of sports were becoming recognized, governing bodies were set up and clear game rules were written for everyone to follow.

After this, sports like soccer and cricket spread, national and international competitions were held, and the Olympic Games made a comeback! It didn't take long for competitive sport to become hugely popular all over the world.

At first, women and people with physical or intellectual disabilities were barred from most national and international contests. But competitive and recreational sports today are open to everyone – male and female, non-disabled or disabled.

This book explores the world's best-known team and individual sports – from their origins, to their rules, scoring systems, top championships and iconic sportspeople. Find out, too, how your body responds to exercise and how sport science and technology affect modern sports, and enable human athletes to break more records than ever before.

Each topic has a page to read as fast as you like for a speedy grasp of the facts. If you're in a real hurry, you can read the 3-second sum-up instead. Each full-page illustration gives you a colourful at-a-glance guide, too. Then, if you have a few minutes to spare, there are extra facts to discover and hands-on activities to try.

When you've finished, don't be surprised if you find yourself heading for a playing field or sports hall!

About sport

You may play sport, but have you ever wondered where sport originated and what sports the first athletes took part in? This chapter tells you about the history, development and future of sport, and why people are motivated to take part in it. You can also discover how sport has changed over time into an activity that almost anyone can take part in, regardless of where they live, their age or their ability.

About sport
Glossary

adaptive sport A version of a sport that has been adjusted so that people with physical or intellectual disabilites can take part.

Ancient Egypt A powerful civilization that flourished in North Africa from 3000 BCE and lasted around 3,000 years.

Ancient Greece A society that flourished on the Greek mainland and islands, and the surrounding area, from around 800 BCE to 30 BCE.

Athlete A sportsperson who is skilled in their field.

British Empire The group of countries ruled over by the United Kingdom.

event An individual contest or game in a sport. For example, a 100-metre men's sprint in running, or a mixed-doubles match in tennis.

Fun Run A non-competitive running race that anyone can take part in, usually to raise funds for charity.

life skills Positive skills, such as making decisions and supporting other people, that will help you to live a better life.

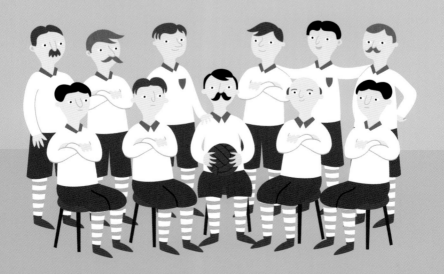

martial art A type of fighting sport, like fencing or wrestling, between individuals. Also called a combat sport.

Middle Ages The time in history from 500 to 1500 CE.

nutrition The nourishment (food and drink) that keeps your body healthy and the way in which your body processes it.

Olympic Games The world's top international sports contest, in which over 200 nations compete. The Games feature a range of summer and winter sports and are divided into Summer and Winter Games. Both are held every four years, but two years apart.

performance enhancing drugs Illegal medication that acts on the body in certain ways, such as making muscles bigger, or increasing the amount of oxygen available.

prehistoric The time before history was written down.

sport science A science that studies how the human body moves and responds to different types of exercise.

sports technology The development of equipment and materials to improve sports performance and training.

How old is sport?

... in 30 seconds

People have played sport for thousands of years. Prehistoric cave paintings of wrestlers and sprinters have been found, and sport contests were an important part of Ancient Egyptian life. Over two thousand years ago, in 776 BCE, the Ancient Greeks held the first Olympic Games.

During the Middle Ages, mainly wealthy people took part in organized sports. Usually, these were combat sports that showed off their fighting skills, like archery and jousting. Poorer people played team ball games like soccer for fun. But there were hardly any rules, and matches often ended in a fight!

In the 19th century, sport was becoming open to everyone. Strict rules were set for soccer, rugby and cricket in Britain, and these team sports were introduced to countries in the British Empire. Martial art sports, like karate and judo, came from Asia to the West, and lacrosse and baseball began in the USA. In 1896, the first modern Olympic Games took place.

Although women and girls played sports, until the 20th century they were often banned from competitions. Today – except in a few societies – women compete in most Olympic events, as well as in most top sports.

3-second sum-up

Sports contests have been popular since prehistoric times.

The oldest sports

These familiar sports began thousands of years old.

Wrestling	7000 BCE
Long jump and javelin	2000 BCE
Hurling (hockey)	980 BCE
Running and discus	706 BCE
Harpastum (rugby)	200 BCE

For centuries, people around the world have taken part in all kinds of competitive sports.

Wrestling is one of the oldest sports of all. Pictures of contests have been found dating back to ancient times.

In the Middle Ages, combat sports like jousting and fencing were a popular pastime for rich nobles.

Top team sports, like soccer, cricket and baseball, began in the 19th century.

Until the 20th century, female sports stars were rare. Suzanne Lenglen was one of the first to gain international fame as a tennis player in the 1910s and 1920s.

Why do people play sport?

... in 30 seconds

Sport isn't just about winning or losing. It rewards everyone who takes part, however good or bad a player they are. You probably know already that exercise improves your health and strength, which helps prevent illnesses. But did you know that sport makes you feel good and gives you essential life skills, too?

Playing sport builds self-confidence and is a great way to make new friends. It can help you to cope with big changes – like moving to a different neighbourhood or starting a new school. Winning is great fun and far easier to deal with than losing. Taking part in sport teaches you respect for others, and how to win and lose well.

In team sports, players work together to score points and win the game. Although each team member is responsible for their own actions, they need to support and work with their team mates, too.

Science shows that playing sport may also make you brainier! When you exercise, the amount of oxygen your body takes in increases. The more oxygen that reaches your brain, the more alert you are.

3-second sum-up

Sport keeps us fit, healthy and happy, and is a fun way to learn important life skills.

What a sport!

German athlete Lutz Long showed true sportsmanship at the 1936 Olympic Games. He had broken a record in the qualifying round for the long jump final and was on course to win gold. When he saw the American athlete, Jesse Owens, fail two attempts to qualify, Lutz suggested he should change his take-off point. Owens succeeded on the third attempt – and went on to win gold in the final.

Playing sport is fun. It's also good for fitness, friendship, confidence and learning!

Regular exercise improves your health and builds up muscles.

Playing a team sport helps you work with other people and is a great way to make new friends.

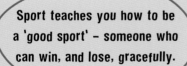

Sport teaches you how to be a 'good sport' – someone who can win, and lose, gracefully.

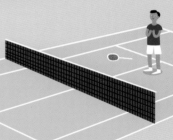

Activity increases blood flow and carries more oxygen to your brain, making you more alert.

Sport for all

... in 30 seconds

You don't need to be a super fit athlete to enjoy sport. Whatever your age or ability you can play your favourite sport in the park, at school or by joining a club. You can take part in sports competitions, too.

Sports facilities like soccer pitches, skateboard parks and cycle tracks are open to everyone. And it's easier than ever to go running, swimming or ice-skating whenever you want. Outdoor table tennis tables have even been set up in some city centres for everyone to use.

A lot of familiar sports have been adapted, so that they can be played by disabled people. These adaptive sports often use special equipment, for example, lightweight racing wheelchairs, or mono skis that are designed for sitting on instead of standing. In many sports contests, certain events are open to people of all abilities. These inclusive events allow people with and without disabilities to compete with each other.

The way we think about sport has changed a lot. At one time, we thought that only the best sportsmen and sportswomen should be allowed to enter competitive sport. Today we realise how important it is for people of all ages and abilities to enjoy it.

3-second sum-up

Today, everyone is encouraged to take part in sports events, whatever their ability.

Beat that!

Older athletes can still be winners, as these achievements show:

- At 90, Mavis Lindgren ran a marathon in 8 hours 53 minutes.
- 100 year-old Fauja Singh ran 100 metres in 23.4 seconds.
- At 105, Robert Marchand cycled a world-record distance of 22.6 km in one hour.

Future sport

... in 30 seconds

Today more people than ever watch and play all kinds of sports. The invention of television in the 20th century allowed millions to view exciting sports events, such as the Olympic Games, for the first time. Televising popular sports like soccer, cricket and basketball worldwide made them even more popular.

The development of the bicycle and the car led to a different type of sport, in which the human body controls a machine. New technology continues to affect sport, and scientists today are working on ways to make future sportspeople fitter, faster and stronger. By focussing on training, nutrition and recovery time, and on materials used for clothing, footwear and playing surfaces, sport science is striving to improve human performance.

No one really knows what the limits of human athletes are, but it can be fun to speculate. For example, the world's fastest sprinters are capable of running 100 metres in 10 seconds – a speed slightly faster than 22 mph/ 35 kph. If, one day, this pace could be kept up for longer, it would mean an athlete could run a mile (1.6 km) in 2 minutes 41 seconds, and a marathon (42 km) in just 1 hour 10 minutes!

3-second sum-up

As sport science and technology advances so will human achievement.

Drugs in sport

Being the best and always winning is so important to some sportspeople and their coaches, that they cheat and use illegal drugs to improve their performance. This is why all competitors are tested for traces of drugs in their blood or urine. If they are found, the sportsperson faces a long ban from their sport.

Scientific advances in equipment, training and fitness enable sportspeople to achieve better performances.

Scientists develop new sportswear fabrics, such as swimwear that mimics a shark's skin, so that it cuts down drag.

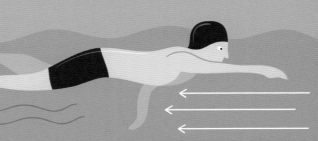

Drag is the force that pushes against a swimmer and slows them down.

Virtual Reality allows sportspeople to improve their skills even when they are training alone.

It's thought that the success of prosthetic body technology – such as running blades worn by disabled athletes – might even lead to the development of artificial sportspeople!

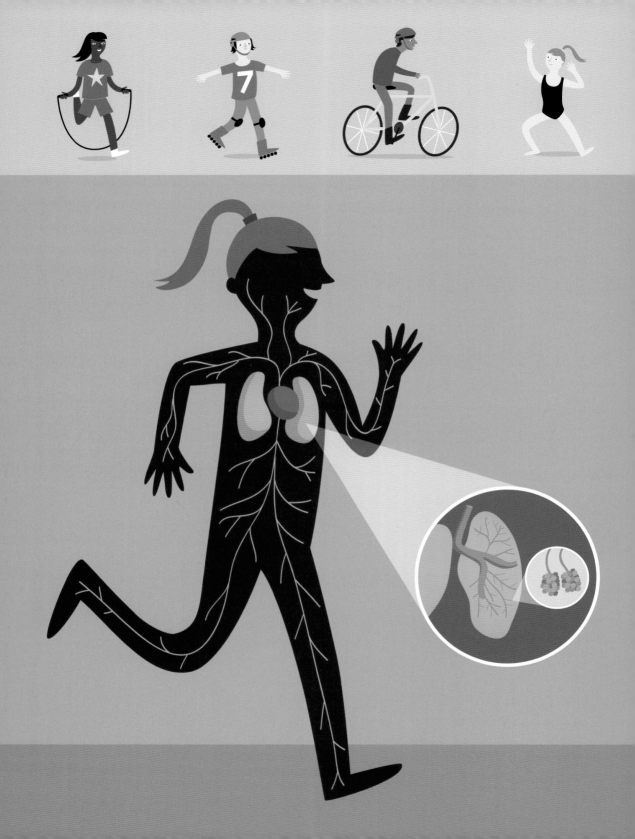

Sport science

For many years, scientists have been researching how the human body changes during sport. Whether a long endurance activity, or an intense, fast burst of effort, our remarkable heart, lungs and muscles adapt to the demands required. Using this knowledge, sport scientists can work with coaches and athletes to design the most effective training programmes for their sport.

Sport science
Glossary

aerobic system A slow process that makes large amounts of energy from the oxygen, carbohydrate and fat we take into our bodies

anaerobic system A process for producing energy quickly from carbohydrate stored in our muscles, without using oxygen.

arteries Large blood vessels that carry oxygen-rich blood from the lungs to our muscles.

blood vessels The hollow tubes that carry blood around the body, transporting oxygen and nutrients to organs, cells and muscles.

breathing rate The number of breaths we take in and out each minute.

carbohydrates A group of nutrients in foods used by the body to make energy.

circulatory system The body system made up of the heart, blood and blood vessels that carries oxygen and nutrients around the body and takes away harmful waste.

evaporate To change from a liquid form into vapour – a form of gas.

fat A group of nutrients in foods that the body uses to make energy.

lactic acid A substance created in the muscles during anaerobic activity that causes fatigue.

lungs The two large organs in your chest that fill with air when you breathe in.

marathon A long-distance running race over about 42 km (26.2 miles).

moisture-wicking fabric Material that pulls sweat away from the skin and onto its surface, so that it can evaporate.

muscles Bands of tissue made up of stretchy fibres that help us move and stay alive.

nervous system The body system made up of the brain and spinal cord, which sends instructions from your brain to different parts of your body, and vice versa.

nutrients The substances in the food we eat – such as carbohydrates and fats – that keep the body active and healthy.

oxygen A gas in the air we breathe.

prosthetic An artificial body part, such as a leg, hand or arm.

Virtual Reality Artificial sights and sounds created by a computer that people experience through a headset, and can interact with.

Aerobic energy
... in 30 seconds

Your body needs energy to play sport. You get this energy from the carbohydrates and fat in the food you eat. These are stored in your muscles and the liver and, when activity starts, they join up with oxygen to release energy. This way of producing energy enables aerobic activity – like swimming or cycling – which can be done for long periods of time.

Inside our lungs, the oxygen we breathe in travels through the walls of millions of tiny air sacs into a network of minute blood vessels called capillaries. From here, the oxygen starts its journey to the muscles.

The powerful action of the heart pumps the oxygen-rich blood around the body through large blood vessels called arteries. At the muscles, the wide arteries divide into narrow capillaries, with walls that are thin enough to allow the oxygen to move into the muscles. Here, the oxygen combines with fat or carbohydrates to produce energy.

Oxygen makes up around one-fifth of the air we breathe. You usually take 12 to 18 breaths a minute, and around 4 to 6 litres of air enters your lungs. During exercise, our breathing rate increases to let in more oxygen. During heavy exercise, top sportspeople can take up to 50 breaths a minute.

3-second sum-up

During activity, oxygen combines with stored carbohydrates and fat to release energy.

3-minute mission Breath count

Sit quietly and find your pulse. Using a timer, count how many beats you feel in one minute. Then count the number of breaths you take in one minute.

Quickly walk five times up and down a flight of stairs. Take your pulse and count your breaths again.

What do you notice?

Oxygen combines with carbohydrates and fat to produce the energy you need for long-term exercise.

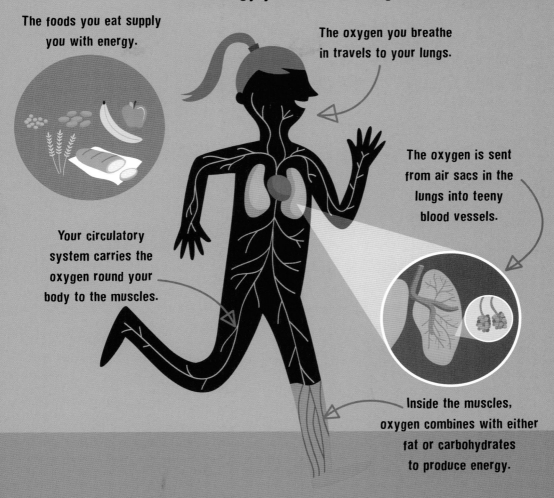

The foods you eat supply you with energy.

The oxygen you breathe in travels to your lungs.

The oxygen is sent from air sacs in the lungs into teeny blood vessels.

Your circulatory system carries the oxygen round your body to the muscles.

Inside the muscles, oxygen combines with either fat or carbohydrates to produce energy.

These are all types of exercise that use aerobic energy.

Skipping

Rollerblading

Cycling

Dancing

Karate

Anaerobic energy

... in 30 seconds

When energy is needed really fast – for example when sprinting, pushing in a rugby scrum, or making a tennis serve – your body has to produce it without oxygen, using its anaerobic system.

Like the aerobic system, the fuel that provides the energy is found in our food. But fat cannot provide energy at a rapid enough rate, so the anaerobic system uses only the carbohydrate stored in the muscles.

Although the anaerobic system produces energy fast, your muscles quickly tire. This is because a by-product, called lactic acid, is also being produced in the muscles and blood. The rising levels of lactic acid make it harder to produce more energy, and cause the muscles to become painful and tired.

Even the fittest sportspeople find rapid, anaerobic activity difficult to keep up for very long. Not only is it very tiring, it is also harder to stay coordinated, so that you play badly, or miss a shot. When all your energy is exhausted, your body transports more blood and oxygen to the muscles to remove the lactic acid, and it can take many minutes for levels to return to normal.

3-second sum-up

Fast anaerobic energy is produced in your muscles.

Anaerobic marathon

A sprinter who can run 100 metres in 10 seconds would be capable of running a marathon in just 70 minutes ... as long as they continued to produce energy anaerobically, and their lactic acid level stayed the same!

The body can produce short bursts of energy without oxygen using the anaerobic system.

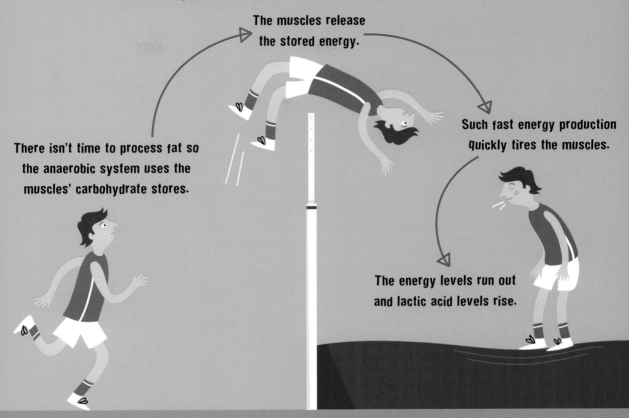

The muscles release the stored energy.

There isn't time to process fat so the anaerobic system uses the muscles' carbohydrate stores.

Such fast energy production quickly tires the muscles.

The energy levels run out and lactic acid levels rise.

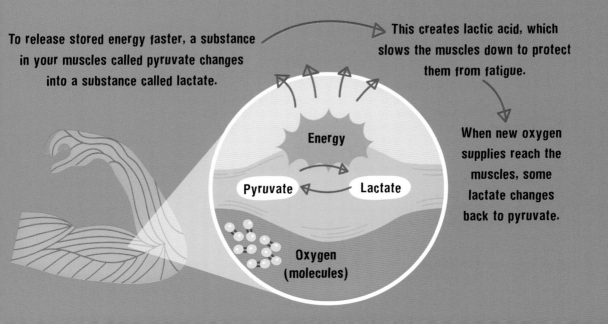

To release stored energy faster, a substance in your muscles called pyruvate changes into a substance called lactate.

This creates lactic acid, which slows the muscles down to protect them from fatigue.

When new oxygen supplies reach the muscles, some lactate changes back to pyruvate.

Energy

Pyruvate

Lactate

Oxygen (molecules)

Muscle power

... in 30 seconds

Three kinds of muscles keep your body working. Cardiac muscle is unique and found only in the walls of your heart. It works automatically, pumping blood and oxygen around your body, and it doesn't tire. Smooth muscles are in the walls of organs like your stomach and intestines. These muscles also work all the time without your noticing.

The third type of muscles – skeletal muscles – move your body around. Skeletal muscles are voluntary, meaning that you control them. Whenever you make a decision to move, signals from your brain whizz through your nervous system to the muscles involved to trigger the movement.

Each skeletal muscle is made up of separate bundles of muscle fibres. Every muscle fibre is also made up of bundles of tiny, slender threads called myofibrils. In their turn, the myofibrils consist of bundles of overlapping, microscopic filaments.

These filaments are divided into separate units called sarcomeres, which are joined to their neighbours at both ends like a string of sausages. When the signal to move arrives from the brain, the overlapping filaments inside the sarcomeres shrink. This shortens the muscle fibres and the muscle contracts, causing movement.

3-second sum-up

Your body has three kinds of muscles: cardiac, smooth and skeletal.

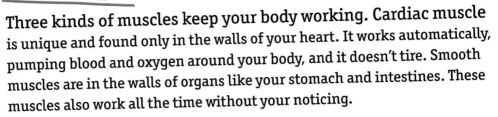

3-minute mission: Blind balance

In a clear space, close your eyes and stand on one leg. Count how long you can stay balanced before you need to lower your leg. Try twice more and see if you can balance for a longer count each time.

Practice daily for two weeks and you should be able to balance for longer. This is because all your muscles will have learnt how to work together, to keep you stable.

Your three muscle types are constantly
working to keep your body on the move.

Signals travel from your
brain to operate your
skeletal muscles.

Your stomach and
other organs are
made of smooth
muscle.

Cardiac muscle is
only in the heart.

Skeletal muscles
are attached
to your bones.

Skeletal muscle is made up of
bundles of tightly packed fibres.

Each muscle fibre is made up
of bundles of myofibrils, divided
into units called sarcomeres.

Body temperature

... in 30 seconds

Our body temperature at rest is 37.0° Celsius. But as soon as exercise starts, the production of energy in our muscles also creates heat, which raises the body's temperature. To keep this rise to a safe level, the body has to lose heat.

One of the main ways the body loses the heat produced by exercise is by sweating. Sweat is a watery fluid produced in sweat glands all over your body. When you sweat, tiny openings in the skin secrete sweat droplets onto the skin surface, where they evaporate.

There is a second method the body uses to keep its temperature stable. Sending more blood to the body's surface – the skin – means that heat can escape to the air outside. The blood vessels just below the skin widen to let more blood flow through them. This is why people can look red when they are exercising.

Overheating and dehydration are dangerous. Sportspeople are careful to drink plenty of fluids to replace the sweat they lose and to wear moisture-wicking sport clothing that helps sweat to evaporate.

3-second sum-up

Activity raises body temperature. Sweating and increased blood flow cools you down.

3-minute mission: Capillary action

See how capillary action in plants inspired moisture-wicking sportwear.

1. Cut the end off a thirsty celery stalk and place it in a glass of water with a few drops of food colouring.

2. Check the stalk over the next few days to see how far up the colour has moved. Coloured dots at the top of the stalk means the water is at the top of the capillaries; when the colour reaches the leaves, the water has evaporated.

Your body is equipped with an efficient cooling system to prevent overheating.

Activity causes the body to heat up.

Turning red shows that hot blood is escaping to the surface.

Sweating produces watery droplets that evaporate from your skin.

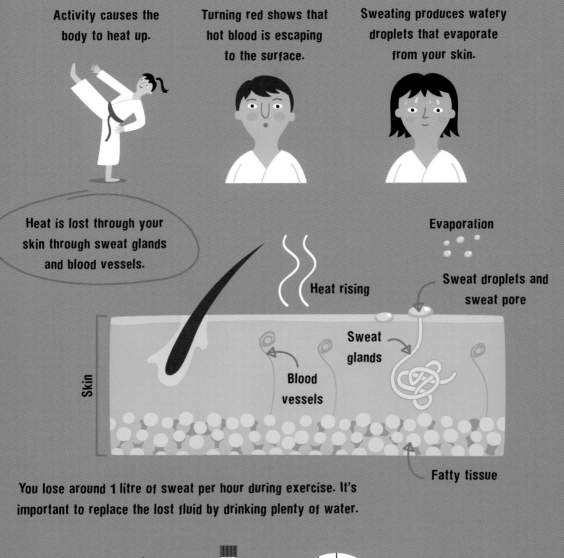

Heat is lost through your skin through sweat glands and blood vessels.

Evaporation

Heat rising

Sweat droplets and sweat pore

Sweat glands

Blood vessels

Skin

Fatty tissue

You lose around 1 litre of sweat per hour during exercise. It's important to replace the lost fluid by drinking plenty of water.

The Olympics

From its origins in Ancient Greece, the Olympic Games has become one of the biggest global events in the sporting calendar. Taking part in an Olympics, and winning an Olympic title, is seen by many sportspeople as the peak of their career. Today's Summer and Winter Olympic and Paralympic Games involve almost every nation in the world. They are very different to the Ancient Olympics, where only Greeks were allowed to compete in just a small number of events.

The Olympics
Glossary

adaptive sport A version of a sport that has been adjusted so that people with physical or intellectual disabilites can take part.

Ancient Greece A society that flourished on the Greek mainland and islands, and the surrounding area, from around 800 BCE to 30 BCE.

Baron Pierre de Coubertin A 19th-century French educator who believed in the value of sport in schools. He set up the International Olympic Committee in 1894.

chariot racing An Ancient Olympic equestrian sport where contestants raced around an oval track. The driver stood in a two-wheeled cart pulled by two or four horses.

discus throw A track-and-field event dating back to the Ancient Olympics, in which athletes compete to see who can throw a discus (heavy disc) the furthest.

IOC (International Olympic Committee) The organization set up by Pierre de Coubertin in 1894 to encourage Olympic values worldwide and the regular celebration of the Olympic Games.

IPC (International Paralympic Committee) The organization set up in 1989 to promote paralympic values and the regular celebration of the Paralympic Games.

javelin throw A track-and-field event dating back to the Ancient Olympics, in which athletes compete to throw a spear-like stick the furthest.

marathon A long-distance running race over about 42 km (26.2 miles).

mascot A person, object or animal that brings good luck.

Mount Olympus The highest mountain peak in Greece, which the Ancient Greeks believed was where their gods lived, ruled over by Zeus.

Olympiad The four-year period between Olympic Games.

Olympic Truce A period of peace so that everyone attending the Ancient Greek Games could travel there and back safely.

pentathlon An Olympic sport made up of five separate events. The Ancient Olympic events were the stade, wrestling, long jump, javelin and discus. The modern events are fencing, swimming, show jumping and Laser-Run (laser pistol shooting and 800-metre run).

Ancient Olympic Games

... in 30 seconds

The first Olympic games were held in 776 BCE in Ancient Greece to honour the Greek god Zeus, the ruler of the gods of Mount Olympus. Athletes from all over Greece came to compete in the Games. The athletes had to be Greek, and travelled to the Games under an 'Olympic Truce', so they could reach the Olympiad safely.

We only know about one sport in the earliest Ancient Olympics. This was a 192-metre sprint called the stade. Later Olympic events included the diaulos, a sprint race twice the distance of the stade, and a 5-km run. Throwing events, like javelin and discus, were added later, along with boxing and wrestling, chariot racing and the multi-event pentathlon.

The Games were held in a stadium and were watched by thousands of spectators, who slept in tents or out in the open. In the evening, there was a feast, which was a bit like a massive barbecue.

On the final day of the Games, the winners were crowned with olive wreaths. When they returned home they were treated like heroes. Women, however, were not allowed to compete in the Games, and only unmarried women could watch.

3-second sum-up

Only Greek athletes competed in the Ancient Olympics, which honoured the chief Greek god Zeus.

Who was Nike?

If the name Nike makes you think of sportswear, think again! To the Ancient Greeks, Nike was the goddess of victory and defender of Zeus. Her picture has appeared on one side of the Olympic medal since 1896, carrying a palm branch for peace and holding up a wreath ready to crown winners.

The Games were held to honour the god Zeus. Athletes came to Olympia from all over Greece.

Discus throwing was a pentathlon event, along with javelin, long jump, the stade and wrestling.

Fire was sacred to the Ancient Greeks and a flame was kept burning for the duration of the Games.

The stade was a sprint held in the stadion (stadium). The race was started by a trumpet blow.

Exciting four-horse and two-horse chariot races were held in the hippodrome, watched by hundreds of spectators.

Modern Olympics
... in 30 seconds

In 1890, Baron Pierre de Coubertin visited a local sports event in Shropshire, England, called the Wenlock Olympian Games. De Coubertin, who was a strong supporter of sport, was so impressed with what he saw that he decided to establish the International Olympic Committee (IOC), and to recreate a modern version of the Ancient Olympics.

Baron Pierre de Coubertin

In 1896, the IOC organized the first modern Olympics in Olympia in Greece. There were 241 athletes from 14 nations participating. Ever since – apart from breaks for the two World Wars – the Olympic Games have taken place every four years in different cities around the world. In 1924, the Winter Olympics were introduced.

Over 4,000 athletes from almost every nation in the world compete in the modern Olympics. Like the Ancient Games, the winners don't receive prize money. Instead they are awarded a gold medal and the honour of becoming an Olympic Champion.

As well as overseeing the Games, the IOC is responsible for encouraging Olympic values – such as excellence, respect, peace, friendship and equality – through sport.

3-second sum-up

The first modern Games took place in 1896. The Olympic values are the same as they were in the original Games.

The Olympic flag

The five linked rings on the Olympic flag, represent each of the five continents that participated in the games when the flag was designed in 1912. The five colours – red, yellow, blue, green and black on a white background – were chosen because at least one of these colours appears on the flag of every nation in the world.

This timeline shows some of the key events in the journey of the modern Olympic Games.

1896 ATHENS, GREECE. First modern Olympic Games.

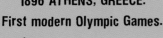

1904 ST LOUIS, USA. Gold, silver and bronze medals first awarded.

1916 Games cancelled due to World War 1.

1924 CHAMONIX, FRANCE. First Winter Olympics. Introduction of Olympic motto: **FASTER, HIGHER, STRONGER.**

'...I promise that we shall take part in these Olympic Games, respecting and abiding by the rules which govern them...in the true spirit of sportsmanship...'

1920 Olympic flag and Olympic oath introduced.

1936 BERLIN, GERMANY. First relay of the Olympic torch and first televised Games.

1940 & 1944 Games cancelled due to World War 2.

1948 STOKE MANDEVILLE HOSPITAL, UK. First disabled Games.

2020 TOKYO, JAPAN. Home to the 32nd Olympic Games.

2012 LONDON, UK. First Games with female competitors from every participating country.

1968 MEXICO CITY, MEXICO. Olympic mascot introduced.

The Winter Olympics

... in 30 seconds

The first Olympic Games for ice and snow sports was held at Chamonix, in the French Alps, in 1924. Five sports were included – bobsleigh, Nordic skiing, skating, curling and ice hockey – and 258 competitors from 16 nations took part.

Ski jumping was the highlight event of the Chamonix Games. This thrilling sport was almost unknown outside Scandinavia at the time, and it caused a sensation. The winning leap by Norwegian skier, Jacob Tulin Thams, was 71 metres – today's champion ski jumpers can reach over 100 metres.

After this, other exciting sports were quickly added to the Winter Olympics. They included short track speed skating, Alpine skiing, luge and skeleton. Today, the Olympics organizers update events constantly to keep the Winter Games popular. Freestyle skiing, snowboarding and moguls are among the latest additions.

Like the Summer Games, the Winter Olympics are held every four years. At first they were held in the same year as the Summer Games, but since 1996 they have been separated by a two-year interval.

3-second sum-up

Ever since the first Winter Olympics introduced audiences to ski jumping, exciting new sports have been part of the Games.

Sonja Henie

One contestant at the 1924 Winter Olympics was only 11 years old! Sonja Henie was from Norway and already a champion skater at home. Unfortunately, at the Chamonix Games she came last in her event – the ladies' figure skating. But she made up for it by winning gold at the next three Winter Olympics and becoming a world-famous sports celebrity.

The first Winter Olympics took place over 90 years ago and featured just five sports. Today there are three times as many.

Ski jumpers at the 1924 games wore thick woollen clothing and used heavy wooden skis.

Olympic skiers today stay warm and dry in high-tech fabrics, and use skis made of lightweight materials.

The Winter Games nowadays has more women competitors than ever, and exciting events like freestyle skiing, bobsleigh and speed skating.

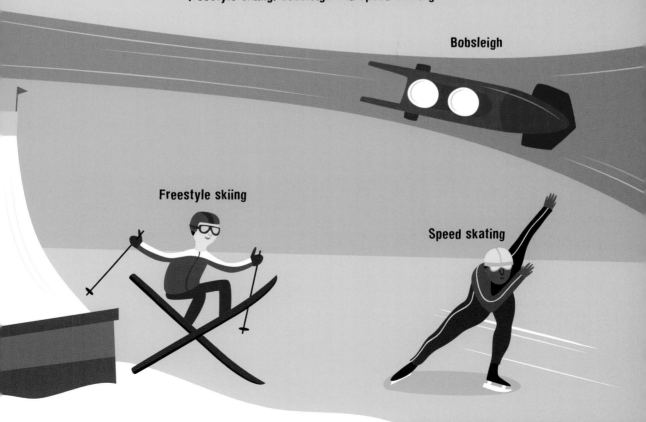

Bobsleigh

Freestyle skiing

Speed skating

The Paralympics

... in 30 seconds

In 1948, in the UK, 16 wheelchair athletes competed in an archery contest, called the Stoke Mandeville Games. These Games, which coincided with the 1948 London Olympics, were the idea of Dr Ludwig Guttmann, and the athletes were paralysed servicemen. From then on, the Stoke Mandeville Games took place every four years after the Summer Olympics, and attracted disabled athletes from all over the world.

In 1960, the first international Stoke Mandeville Games took place in Rome, one week after the Summer Olympics. They were organized by the International Paralympic Committee (IPC), which later renamed them the Paralympic Games. Unfortunately, the 400 disabled athletes had to stay in flats built on stilts, and soldiers had to be drafted in to carry them up and down the steps!

Today, the Winter and Summer Paralympics are two of the largest multi-event competitions in the world. The focus of the Games is on celebrating achievements, and the adapted sports the athletes compete in must fulfill the IPC's vision, which is: 'To enable Para athletes to achieve sporting excellence and inspire and excite the world.'

3-second sum-up

The Paralympic Games celebrates the achievements of disabled men and women.

The Deaflympics

In 1924, athletes from nine countries travelled to Paris, France, to take part in an unusual sports contest. The International Silent Games was the first international sports event for deaf athletes. The contest takes place at four-year intervals, and is the longest-running international sports competition after the Olympic Games. It became known as the Deaflympics in 2001.

Archery was the first paralympic sport.
Today over 4,000 athletes compete in 20 sports.

Paralympic athletes compete in events according to their disability. Events include:

VISUALLY IMPAIRED

Equestrian

5-a-side soccer

Judo

PHYSICALLY IMPAIRED

Road cycling

Wheelchair basketball

Canoe

INTELLECTUALLY IMPAIRED

Swimming

Athletics

Badminton

Injured servicemen competed at archery in the Stoke Mandeville Games of 1948.

Unusual sports

... in 30 seconds

After each Olympiad, the International Olympic Committee decides which sports to keep in the Games and whether to add new ones. Some sports, like track and field, or cycling, include many events. So new events might also be added to or taken out of sports that stay in the Games.

Twelve sports have been dropped from the Games since the 1896 Olympics. Some were unusual! For example, in Tug-of-War, two teams of eight men pulled a rope in opposite directions, with the aim of dragging each other a distance of 2 metres over a line.

Two swimming events removed from the early Games were the Underwater Swim and the Plunge for Distance. Competitors in the Plunge had to dive, then cover as much distance as possible underwater without making a stroke. It was dropped when the IOC realized the heavier competitors had an unfair advantage, as their weight naturally propelled them further.

Motorboating was one of the most disastrous Olympic events. It was held once in 1908. The boats had engines but only reached 30 kph, six of the nine races had to be cancelled due to bad weather, and the races that went ahead were too far from the coast for spectators to watch.

3-second sum-up

Some surprising sports were once part of the modern Olympics.

3-minute mission Olympic events quiz

Can you guess which three unusual events in this list were not part of the early Olympics?

Firefighting
Hopping
Rope climbing
One-legged balance

Stone throwing
Horse long jump
Singing
Poodle clipping

Answers on page 96

The early Olympics featured sports that would be out of place in a modern Games.

The Plunge dive was dropped because it favoured heavier contestants.

In 1908, the British Tug-of-War team's heavy boots got stuck in the ground.

Running Deer shooting was an Olympic event until 1948. The deer was a wooden model that rolled along a track.

Bad weather cancelled most races in the 1908 motorboat event, while others were too far from shore to be properly seen.

Team ball sports

Schools, towns and countries create different-size communities. A major reason for developing team sports is to represent these communities. Some team ball sports, like soccer, have global popularity, whereas others, like volleyball and American Football, are especially popular in certain areas. Team sizes and rules vary from sport to sport, but games between opponents are all played for possession of a ball.

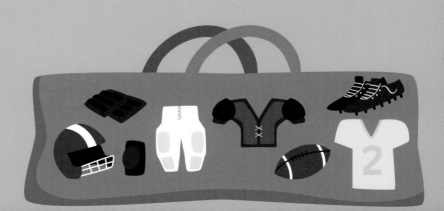

Team ball sports
Glossary

attacking play Playing with the aim of scoring a goal or winning points. Also called offensive play.

coach The person who trains a team of sportspeople.

court A playing area marked out for a ball game, such as basketball, volleyball or tennis.

defensive play Playing with the aim of blocking the attacking side to stop them scoring or winning points.

field Natural or artificial grass area where sports such as soccer or baseball are played. Also called a pitch.

FIFA (International Federation of Association Football) The governing body for soccer and organizer of the men's and women's World Cup championships.

fly-half Key player in a rugby union team who directs attacking play and is skilled at kicking and passing.

half One of two periods of play in a timed game.

match A name for a contest or game between opposing teams or two players.

offside The position of a soccer player who is closer to the opponent's goal line than the ball and the next-to-last opponent.

opponent The person or team on the opposite side in a contest or game.

playoff A series of games to decide which two teams will play in a championship final.

qualifying match A match played between two teams to see which of them will progress to the next level.

quarter One of four periods of play in a timed game.

quarterback An American football player who directs the team's attacking play.

referee The chief official who watches a contest closely to ensure that players follow the rules, and who can stop play if necessary. Also known as an umpire.

serve Hitting a ball at the start of a game.

tackle To try to take the ball from your opponent.

tactics Planned actions by players to help them win points or stop their opponents.

time-out A short break in a sport often called for by a coach.

touchdown See 'try'.

try Touching the ball down behind the goal line in rugby. It is called a touchdown in American Football.

Soccer
... in 30 seconds

Soldiers in ancient China stayed fit by playing cuju, a game in which a ball was kicked into an open net. Cuju is thought to be the earliest form of soccer, or football as it is widely known. Today, soccer is played by millions of men, women and children and is one of the world's most popular team sports.

Pelé

The game we know now began in Britain in 1835, when the first official rules were set out. Although people had played soccer before then, the matches could get out of control – player numbers were unlimited, carrying the ball was allowed and fighting was common!

The modern sport is governed by FIFA – the International Federation of Association Football. A men's soccer World Cup tournament has been held every four years since 1930. The women's soccer World Cup began in 1991. In both tournaments, national teams play in a series of qualifying matches. The top two teams then compete in the final for the honour of becoming world champions.

Edson Arantes do Nascimento – or Pelé – was one of the world's best soccer players. He scored 77 times in 92 appearances for Brazil, including three successful World Cup campaigns. In women's soccer, American player Abby Wambach scored 176 goals, won two Olympic gold medals and a World Cup winner's medal.

3-second sum-up

Modern soccer began in the 19th century and spread around the world.

3-minute mission Kick test

Try this test in a large outdoor space. Aim your kick at the centre of the ball each time.

1. Kick the ball straight ahead.

2. Kick the ball as high as you can.

3. Kick the ball at roughly 45 degrees.

Which angle sends the ball furthest?

The object of soccer is for one team to score more goals than the opposing team. Goals are scored when the ball crosses the goal line between the posts.

90 minutes

 x 11 players per team

 x 1 referee

x 2 assistant referees

The referee looks out for foul play and ensures that players follow the rules.

Assistant referees judge if the ball has gone out of play or if a player is offside.

A team has four types of players: a goalkeeper, defenders, midfielders and strikers.

The strikers are skilled players who can head and kick the ball accurately.

Midfield players are often the busiest players, providing a link between attack and defence.

Defenders help the goalkeeper to protect the goal.

The goal keeper is the only player allowed to touch the ball with their hands and arms.

Ball

Boots

Shirt

Socks

Shorts

Shin guards

Good for:
Aerobic fitness
Cardiovascular health
Muscle strength
Bone strength
Hand-eye coordination
Brain function

Rugby

... in 30 seconds

William Webb Ellis was a pupil at Rugby School in England in 1823. During a soccer match one day, instead of kicking the ball, he picked it up and ran with it! The sport he helped create became popular and was named after the famous school. In 1871, the first official rules were set out.

Maggie Alphonsi

The first rugby balls were made from an air-filled pig's bladder covered in leather. If they got waterlogged, they became heavy and slippery. Today's rugby balls are made of lighter plastic, with a water-resistant surface that is easy to grip. The oval shape of the ball can make it difficult to throw and catch, so players often spin the ball to make it more stable in the air. This unusual shape also causes the ball to bounce in an unpredictable way.

Rugby Union today has grown into a global sport played by millions of people. Every four years, the best nations in the world play in the men's and women's World Cup, with the winners crowned world champions.

New Zealander Dan Carter is thought to be the greatest ever fly-half. He scored 1598 points in 112 games for his country, won the World Cup twice and was voted International Rugby Board Player of the Year three times. Maggie Alphonsi overcame a foot disability to play 74 times for England. She took part in two World Cup championships and was a co-winner of the Six Nations title a record seven times.

3-second sum-up

Rugby was invented by a bored schoolboy. The oval shape of the ball affects how it moves in the air.

The scrum

Certain breaks in play are re-started with a scrum, when the eight forwards in each team bind together to push their opponents backwards and win the ball. The total weight of each set of forwards is about 900 kg – about the same as a small car!

In rugby, the winning team is the one that scores the most points at the end of the game.

80 minutes

x 15 players per team

x 1 referee

x 2 assistant referees

Each team has eight forwards and seven backs who all aim to score a try or a goal.

Kicking the ball over the H-shaped cross-bar is a goal worth 3 points.

Players can only move the ball forwards by kicking it, running with it or moving it inside a scrum.

The ball is passed sideways or backwards to team mates.

Grounding the ball in the opponent's in-goal area is a try worth 5 points.

Opponents tackle the ball carrier, to bring them to the ground.

Good for :
Leg strength
Upper-body strength
Aerobic fitness
Speed

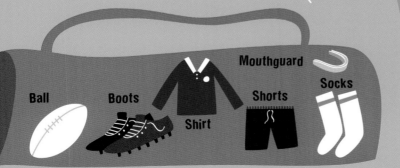
Ball   Boots   Shirt   Mouthguard   Shorts   Socks

Basketball
... in 30 seconds

This sport was invented in 1891 by Canadian P.E. teacher, James Naismith, who was trying to keep his gym class busy on a rainy day. The indoor sport he came up with used wooden peach baskets as hoops and a soccer ball. Players also rubbed coal dust on their hand to grip the ball better!

Basketball grew into one of the most popular team sports of all, especially in the USA. Men's basketball has featured in every Olympic Games since 1936, and women's basketball has been an Olympic sport since 1976, with teams from the USA winning more gold medals than any other nation.

Michael Jordan

International matches are made up of four 10-minute quarters. But the clock is stopped when play is not active, and coaches can call time-outs to discuss tactics. The side in possession of the ball plays an attacking game, changing to defensive play if the ball is lost. A field goal wins 2 points. The 3-point goal is also a field goal but scored from behind the 3-point line. A 'slam dunk' is a goal made by jumping high and shooting the ball down through the hoop.

The best players tend to be tall. Famous US player, Michael Jordan, is 1.98m! Over 15 seasons, his average score per game was more than 30 points. Top female player, Lisa Leslie, won four Olympic gold medals in her 12-year career in the Women's National Basketball Association.

3-second sum-up

The first basketball players aimed a soccer ball at a fruit basket. Today it's a top international sport.

3-minute mission Ball bounce challenge

Find a hard surface and a large ball such as a basketball, soccer ball or netball, and bounce the ball on the ground using one hand. Swap hands and repeat.

Once you can do this, try bouncing the ball while walking. When you can bounce and walk, try bouncing the ball while running!

In a basketball match, the teams score points by throwing the ball through their opponent's basket.

40 minutes

x 5 players per team

x 1 referee

x 2 umpires

A rebound shot is when the ball bounces through the hoop off the backboard.

The arms and shooting hand must be correctly positioned for a good jump shot.

Backboard

46-cm-wide hoop

3-point line

Centre circle

Centre line

Players bounce the ball with their fingertips to move it around and for passing.

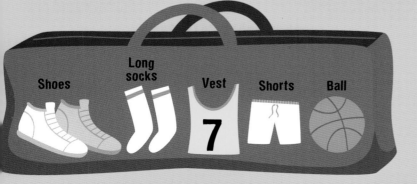

Shoes

Long socks

Vest 7

Shorts

Ball

Good for :
Coordination
Arm strength
Agility
Aerobic fitness
Reactions

Volleyball

... in 30 seconds

This sport came from a popular game that was played in YMCA clubs in the USA, at the end of the 19th century. It quickly became popular across America. A lightweight ball was designed in 1900 for the sport, which spread to Europe around the time of the First World War. The first World Championships were held in 1949, and volleyball became an Olympic sport in 1964.

Misty
May-Treanor

Volleyball is a blend of basketball, handball and tennis. It is played on indoor and outdoor courts and players use their hands to hit the ball over the net. If the team playing the ball allow it to hit the floor, if a player touches the ball twice in a row, or if the ball is hit out of court, their opponents gain a point.

Most matches have a maximum of five sets. The team to reach 25 points, 2 points ahead of their opponents, wins the set. The fifth set is played to just 15 points. A specialist player – the libero – can be brought on at any time into the back row to improve the team's defences.

Retired Brazilian player, Gustavo Endres, won World League, World Championship and Olympic titles, and was often voted 'best blocker' in major tournaments. In 10 years, American beach volleyball player, Misty May-Treanor, won a run of 112 matches and 19 tournaments, including three Olympic and three World Championship gold medals.

3-second sum-up

Volleyball developed from basketball, handball and tennis.

Beach volleyball

Beach volleyball is a version of the sport played on the beach or other sandy surface. Instead of six players there are only two players on each side. It has been played at the Olympics since 1992.

In a volleyball game, the players rotate and change their positions on the court before serving and each time a team wins a point.

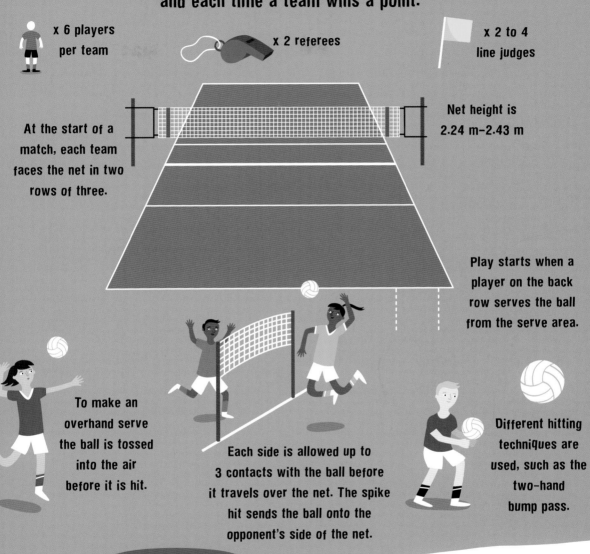

x 6 players per team

x 2 referees

x 2 to 4 line judges

At the start of a match, each team faces the net in two rows of three.

Net height is 2.24 m–2.43 m

Play starts when a player on the back row serves the ball from the serve area.

To make an overhand serve the ball is tossed into the air before it is hit.

Each side is allowed up to 3 contacts with the ball before it travels over the net. The spike hit sends the ball onto the opponent's side of the net.

Different hitting techniques are used, such as the two-hand bump pass.

Ball

Socks

Shorts

Shirt

Trainers

Good for :
Leg strength
Flexibility
Arm strength
Reactions
Coordination

American football

... in 30 seconds

America's favourite sport emerged towards the end of the nineteenth century. By then, rugby and soccer had spread from Britain to the USA and other countries. In America, a rugby coach called Walter Camp developed the first set of rules that changed rugby into American Football.

Joe Montana

In the game, each team aims to move the ball down the field into their opponent's end zone, while defending their own end zone. Play happens in a series of short advances, known as 'downs', where the team with the ball tries to carry it a distance of 9.1 metres, before the defending team can win it back. Points are scored for goals or touchdowns, and the team with the most points wins.

Each year, two winning teams from the NFL (National Football League) compete in the Super Bowl championship final. It is shown on television in 200 countries with an estimated global audience of over 1 billion people.

Women's American Football uses a slightly smaller ball. Sami Grisafe was part of the USA World Championship-winning teams of 2010 and 2013 – she is also an actor and singer! World-famous quarterback, Joe Montana, holds the Super Bowl career record for completing 122 passes without an interception (tackle).

3-second sum-up

This game evolved from rugby and became America's most popular sport.

3-minute mission Weight lift

The protective padded uniform worn by male American footballers can add up to 9 kg to their weight. See what half that amount feels like when you exercise!

You need: 4.5 kg of packet foods • 2 strong bags

Walk up and down a flight of stairs twice. Then divide the packets evenly between the bags. Now walk carefully back up and down the stairs twice carrying the bags.

In American football, the teams battle for the ball in short 'downs'. The side that moves the ball forwards 9.1 metres keeps hold of it for the next down.

60 minutes

x 11 players per team

 x 1 referee

x 1 umpire
x 1 head linesman
x 4 line judges

The 110-metre-long pitch is marked off in 4.6-metre divisions.

Kicking the ball between the posts and over the 3-metre-high crossbar is a field goal, worth 3 points.

Players who reach the end zone make a touchdown to win points.

A touchdown in the opposing end zone is worth 6 points.

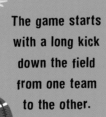

The game starts with a long kick down the field from one team to the other.

Team mates move the ball forwards by passing it or by carrying it in a running play.

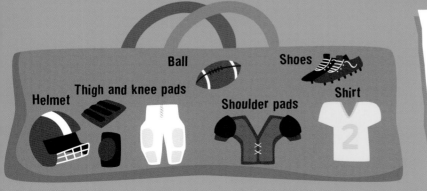

Ball

Shoes

Thigh and knee pads

Shirt

Helmet

Shoulder pads

Good for :
Strength
Speed
Agility
Mental toughness
Coordination

Team ball-and-stick sports

Instead of hands or feet, some team ball sports involve an implement, such as a bat, to pass the ball during the game and to score points and goals against the opposing team. Like most modern sports, the versions of cricket, baseball and hockey that are popular today developed from much earlier ball-and-stick games that were played in different places around the world.

Team ball-and-stick sports
Glossary

bowl To throw the ball towards the batsman in a cricket game.

British Empire The group of countries ruled over by the United Kingdom.

fielder A player who stops or throws a ball hit by an opponent to prevent them from scoring.

innings The period of play in cricket or baseball when one team has a turn at batting.

league A group of teams that arranges matches between its members.

medieval From the time of the Middle Ages – from 500 to 1500 CE.

pitch To throw the ball towards the batter in a baseball game.

play off A series of games to decide which two teams will play in a championship final.

puck A small circular rubber disc, weighing about 170 g, that is used in ice hockey instead of a ball.

Test match An international cricket match that lasts up to five days. It was named a 'Test' match because such a long game is an endurance test for the players.

umpire Another name for a referee, the chief official who watches a contest closely to ensure that players follow the rules, and who can stop play if necessary.

wicket Three upright sticks with two bails (short sticks) balanced on top.

Cricket
... in 30 seconds

Experts think cricket may have started as a children's game in medieval England. A stick or farm tool was used for the bat and a piece of wood or bundle of sheep's wool for the ball. Later, in the 1600s, adults began playing, and by the 1700s, cricket had become an organized team sport.

Claire
Taylor

In a modern match, each side plays an innings, in which the players in one team bat and the players in the other team bowl or field. The batter stops the ball from reaching the wicket behind them by hitting it away. Points called runs are scored, either by running between the two wickets, or by hitting the ball out of the field. A bowler bowls six times – an 'over' – before the ball goes to another bowler, who bowls from the opposite end of the pitch. After one or two innings per side, the team who scores the most runs wins the match.

Cricket became a global sport during the 19th century. In 1877, England played Australia in the first ever Test match, which lasted five days.

Women's international cricket grew from a 1934 match between England and Australia. The most prestigious women's tournament today is a series of one-day matches for the World Cup. The top female players include Claire Taylor, who has been described as the greatest batter in the women's game. In men's cricket, the West Indies player, Garfield Sobers, is recognized as the sport's greatest all-rounder.

3-second sum-up

Cricket grew from a medieval children's game into a top world sport.

The Ashes

When England lost to Australia in 1882, people joked that it was the death of English cricket. The next time England won against Australia, the ashes of a burned bail (a short stick across the top of the wicket) were presented to the English captain. The series of Test matches played between England and Australia has been called 'The Ashes', ever since.

In a cricket match, teams take turns at bowling the ball or at batting it away before it can hit the wicket.

x 11 players per team

x 2-3 umpires

Each team bats for an innings, which ends after a fixed number of overs, or when all of the team are out.

The fielding team take up different positions that are selected by the captain.

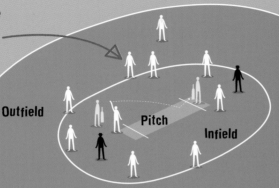

Outfield

Pitch

Infield

There are two batters, one at each end.

Fast bowlers run up to the wicket before releasing the ball at speeds that can reach 161 kph.

Mid-bound

Back foot contact

Front foot contact

Follow through

The batter's position must give them the best chance of defending the wicket and hitting the ball to score runs.

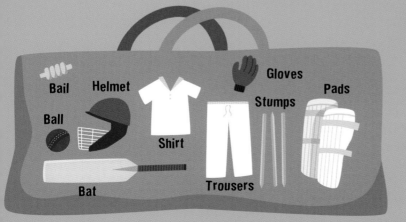

Bail

Helmet

Gloves

Stumps

Pads

Ball

Shirt

Bat

Trousers

Good for :
Strength
Balance
Anticipation
Reactions
Coordination

Baseball
... in 30 seconds

Baseball developed in the USA from bat and ball games that had developed in Europe. In the mid-1800s, the sport was so popular that the American press named it 'the national game'.

Joe DiMaggio

In a game, the sides switch between offense (batting and base running) and defence (pitching and fielding). Players on the batting side stand on the home plate, facing the pitcher who throws the ball from a raised mound. To score runs, the batter must run around the bases and return to the home plate. When three players in a team are out, the innings is over, and the teams swap from offense to defence.

Teams in America compete in two leagues: the Major League Baseball and the American League. Every year, the best teams compete in a series of play offs for the World Series championship. Baseball is also played in Japan, Cuba and Canada, and will be an Olympic sport in 2020.

Joe DiMaggio played for the New York Yankees. He is famous for a 'hitting streak' – striking the ball and reaching first base in 56 consecutive matches. Doris Sams was one of the best players in the history of the All-America Girls Pro-Baseball League.

3-second sum-up

Baseball came from older ball-and-stick games.

Fielding gloves

The gloves worn by fielders are different designs, depending on the playing position. The large fingerless glove – or mitt – worn by the catcher is made of leather and is almost 33 cm wide. To make catching easier it doesn't have fingers. When the pitcher throws the ball, they aim for the mitt. If three pitches are legally caught by the catcher, the batter is out.

A baseball game isn't timed. The two sides take turns at batting and fielding to complete an innings and the game lasts for nine innings.

x 9 players per team

x 1 head umpire

x 1-5 field umpires

When the batter scores a hit they run from base to base. The fielders must catch the ball or throw it to a base to get the batter out.

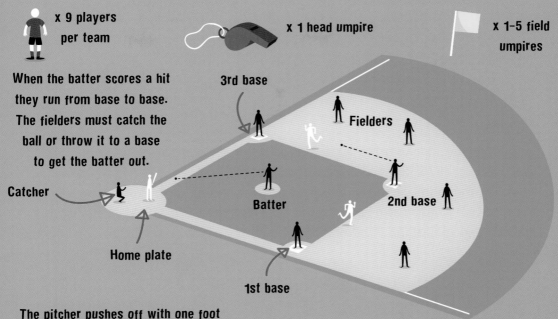

3rd base

Fielders

Catcher

Batter

2nd base

Home plate

1st base

The pitcher pushes off with one foot for a more powerful throw and aims for the catcher's mitt.

The batter has three chances to hit the ball.

The catcher wears a fingerless mitt to make catching the ball easier.

Cap

Fielding glove

Chest protector

Trousers

Helmet

Shirt

Bat

Ball

Good for :
Speed
Strength
Reactions
Coordination

Field hockey and ice hockey
... in 30 seconds

Games that use a curved stick to hit a ball date back thousands of years. Different hockey-style sports were played all over the world. Hurling – a game played in Ireland – was banned in the 1400s because it was so dangerous!

Kate Richardson-Walsh

Modern field hockey started in the UK, where it was played at some schools. In 1876, the official game rules were set out, based on soccer. Hockey was popular in the British Army and quickly spread through the British Empire and the world. At around the same time, ice hockey developed in Canada – today it is the country's national winter sport.

Ice hockey is a variation of field hockey. Instead of a ball, two teams of six players hit a disc called a puck across ice. The action is fast and furious: the puck can rebound at up to 160 kph off the side boards surrounding the pitch, and players wear heavy protective padding. One tactic – body-checking – is a way of stopping an opponent's progress by pushing them into the side boards.

Canadian player Wayne Gretsky has been called the greatest ever ice hockey player. He is the leading scorer in the National Hockey League's history. Kate Richardson-Walsh has played field hockey for England and Great Britain a record 375 times and captained Great Britain in the 2016 Olympics when they won gold.

3-second sum-up

Field and ice hockey came from simple ball-stick games. The modern sports are played internationally.

3-minute mission Frozen bounce

The puck is frozen before an ice hockey game to stop it bouncing too much. You can use four tennis balls to see how temperature affects bounce. Put one ball in the freezer, one in the fridge, one in a warm place and one in a very warm place – in the sun or on top of a radiator. After 1–2 hours, take out and drop one ball at a time to test the height of its bounce.

60 minutes

Field hockey has 11 players on each side and is similar to soccer. Ice hockey is an indoor game with six players on each team.

x 11 players per team

x 2 umpires

Only the flat side of the stick may be used for passing, dribbling and hitting the small, hard ball.

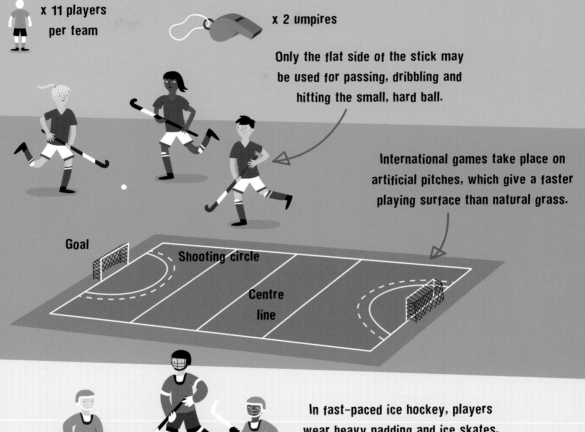

International games take place on artificial pitches, which give a faster playing surface than natural grass.

Goal

Shooting circle

Centre line

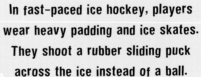

In fast-paced ice hockey, players wear heavy padding and ice skates. They shoot a rubber sliding puck across the ice instead of a ball.

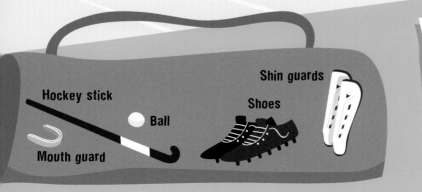

Hockey stick

Ball

Shin guards

Shoes

Mouth guard

Good for :
Flexibility
Upper- and lower-body strength
Speed
Aerobic fitness

Individual sports

Not all sports involve teams of players. In individual sports, players compete against each other. The range of sports in these head-to-head contests call for different physical and mental skills. Some, such as motor racing, require complex equipment, while others, such as track-and-field events, are simple contests of speed, strength and agility.

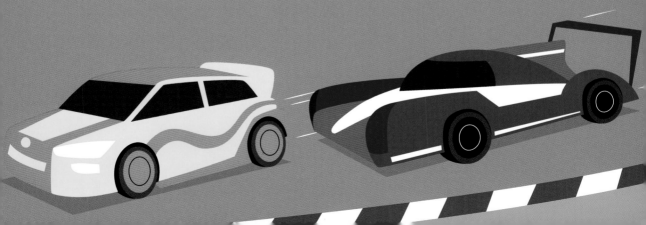

Individual sports
Glossary

aerodynamic Something made in a streamlined shape, so that it moves easily and speedily through air or water. For example, a Formula One racing car.

athleticism An athlete's skills, such as agility, fitness and strength.

chariot racing Ancient Olympic equestrian sport where contestants raced around an oval track. The driver stood in a two-wheeled cart pulled by two or four horses.

club A heavy stick, thicker at one end, used in golf for hitting the ball.

course The playing area for a game of golf.

decathlon A men's track and field contest of 10 events: 100-metre sprint, 110-metre hurdles, 400-metre race, 1500-metre race, long jump, high jump, shot put, discus throw, javelin throw and pole vault.

dressage An equestrian sport where horses and riders carry out precise movements.

equestrian A type of sport for riders on horseback.

fault The name for an action that is against the rules, used in many sports including, tennis, gymnastics and show jumping.

flutter kick A swimming stroke made by moving the legs rapidly up and down.

Grand Slam A set of top international tournaments in one sport, for example tennis or rugby, which are all held in the same year.

heptathlon A women's track-and-field contest of 7 events: 100-metre hurdles, 200-metre sprint, 800-metre race, high jump, shot put, long jump and javelin throw.

lane A narrow strip the length of a swimming pool or running track, that a competitor races inside.

plastron A piece of clothing that fencers wear to protect the chest.

ring The arena for combat sports, such as boxing and wrestling.

scissor kick A swimming stroke where the legs open and close like a frog's.

Spanish Riding School Famous horse-riding school in Vienna, Austria, set up in the 16th century to train Lipizzaner horses (ancestors of Spanish horses) and riders in the Renaissance tradition of riding.

velodrome A track for cycle-racing with steep, banked curves.

wind tunnel A tube-shaped research laboratory where sports engineers and scientists can test the effects of high-speed airflow on racing vehicles, equipment and athletes.

Dressage and show jumping

... in 30 seconds

Humans and horses have had a close relationship for thousands of years. Horses were used in battle and equestrian sports were part of the Ancient Greek Olympics. These events included chariot racing, which tested the horses' stamina and speed, and dressage, which showed their level of training.

Mark Todd

Modern dressage came from a training system developed in 1572 at the Spanish Riding School of Vienna, Austria. It became an Olympic event in 1912, but until 1952 only military officers could compete. Today, dressage is one of the fastest growing Olympic sports. The sport of show jumping grew out of fox hunting, at a time when the British countryside was first divided by fences and hedges. It became an Olympic sport for the first time in 1900.

The world's best riders and horses also compete for an annual World Cup and at the World Equestrian Games, which is held every four years. The New Zealander, Mark Todd, is a champion show jumper who has competed in seven Olympic Games. British dressage rider, Charlotte Dujardin, has won three Olympic dressage gold medals on her horse, Valegro. Together, they have helped make the sport more popular.

3-second sum-up

Equestrian sports like dressage and show jumping are built on trust between horse and rider.

3-minute mission Jump test

Test out three different take off positions to see how your muscles and limbs help you to jump higher.

Take off 1. Arms by your sides and knees bent – JUMP!

Take off 2. Arms by your sides and standing. Bend the knees – JUMP!

Take off 3. Arms by your sides and standing. Bend knees, raise your arms – JUMP!

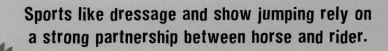

Sports like dressage and show jumping rely on a strong partnership between horse and rider.

Dance-like dressage moves are smooth and precise and both horse and rider have to be very smartly presented.

Show jumpers need good upper body and leg strength. Horse and rider aim for a fault-free round in a set time.

Jump course obstacles are different sizes. They are placed so the horse has to keep changing direction.

Good for :
Leg strength
Upper-body strength
Balance
Flexibility
Concentration

Swimming and diving

... in 30 seconds

Swimming was part of the first modern Olympic Games in 1896. But competitive swimming had begun almost a hundred years earlier, when the most popular swimming stroke was breast stroke.

Guo
Jingjing

In London in 1844, two Native Americans beat two British men in a swimming race, using a crawling stroke. Even though this stroke was clearly faster, British competitors refused to give up breast stroke! By the end of the nineteenth century, a crawling arm stroke with a breast stroke scissor kick was popular. When a flutter kick replaced the scissor kick the modern front crawl was born. After scientists in the 1930s showed how inefficient breaststroke was, butterfly and back stroke were developed, and these four strokes are used in competition swimming around the world.

Diving developed from gymnastics. It became an Olympic event for men in 1904 and for women in 1912. Contestants dive from a 3-metre-high springboard or a 10-metre-high solid platform. In synchronized diving, two divers match each other's movements.

American swimmer, Michael Phelps, has won 23 Olympic gold medals. Guo Jingjing, from China, is one of the world's most successful divers. She started diving aged 6, and has won six Olympic medals.

3-second sum-up

Front crawl is the fastest of the four competitive swimming strokes. Diving is water gymnastics.

3-minute mission Buoyancy test

Swimmers float because their body weighs less than water and their lungs are full of air. But something with more density than the water around it sinks.

You need: 2 oranges – 1 whole, 1 peeled • Jug of water

Put the oranges in the water. The peeled orange should sink below the whole one. The air in the peel of the whole orange makes it less dense, so it floats higher.

Competitive swimming races test speed over short or long distances while diving tests technical agility.

The face-down position lets the arms move freely.

It is faster to move each arm through air than through water.

Pulling forwards using alternate arms in a rolling motion is less tiring than using both arms together.

Breast stroke is the slowest of the four swimming strokes.

Breast stroke is the least efficient because the arms move forwards under the water.

Butterfly is a fish-like stroke that raises both arms out of the water.

In backstroke, the arms do most of the work.

In competition diving, the judges award points based on difficulty and technique.

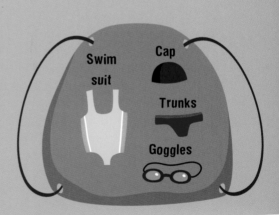

Swim suit

Cap

Trunks

Goggles

A high diver can enter the water at up to 96.5 kph!

Good for :
Aerobic fitness
Strength
Flexibility
Speed
Mental toughness

Track and field

... in 30 seconds

This series of running, throwing and jumping events were inspired by the foot races and throwing contests held in the Ancient Olympic stadium. The track-and-field sports we know today developed in the early 1900s.

Jesse Owens

There are 24 events: the track events are types of running races; the field events include four jumping and four throwing events. In addition, there is the seven-event women's heptathlon and the 10-event men's decathlon. The only running event that doesn't take place on the track is the 26.2-mile (42-km) marathon.

The best athletes compete in regular competitions worldwide. At first, the majority of track-and-field athletes were men. In 1928, 95 women athletes competed for the first time in the Summer Olympics in five events. In the 2016 Summer Games, around a thousand female track-and-field athletes were entered in more than 20 events.

Black American Jesse Owens was the first athlete to gain four gold medals at a single Olympics – the 1936 Berlin Games. In 2000, the Australian 400-metre runner, Cathy Freeman, became Olympic champion. She was the first Aboriginal person ever to win a gold medal.

3-second sum-up

There are 24 running, jumping and throwing events in track and field.

3-minute mission Go skip!

Sportspeople train daily and a skipping workout is often part of the routine. This aerobic exercise can improve:

coordination	bone density	balance
breathing	muscle power	alertness
reflexes	stamina	memory

Try a skipping workout with a friend. Time each other – how many jumps per minute can you do?

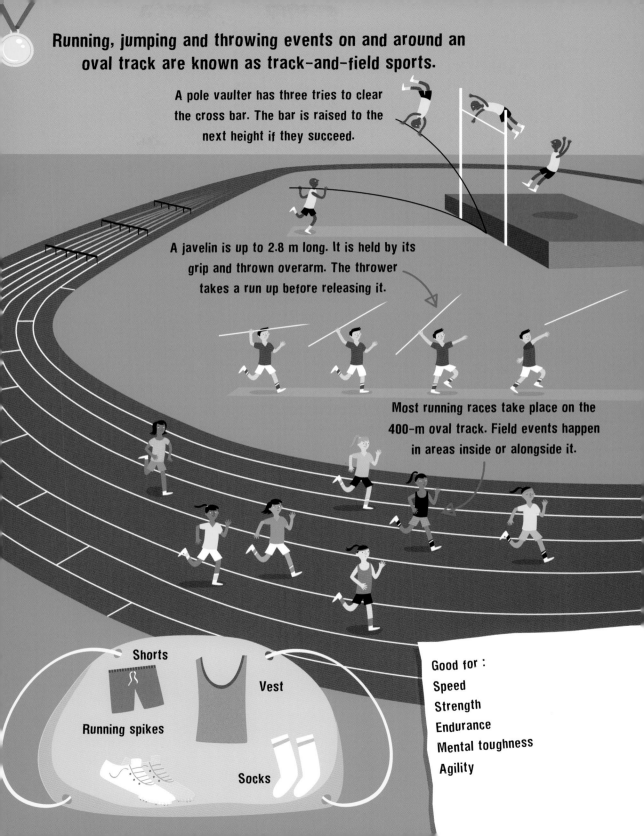

Running, jumping and throwing events on and around an oval track are known as track-and-field sports.

A pole vaulter has three tries to clear the cross bar. The bar is raised to the next height if they succeed.

A javelin is up to 2.8 m long. It is held by its grip and thrown overarm. The thrower takes a run up before releasing it.

Most running races take place on the 400-m oval track. Field events happen in areas inside or alongside it.

Shorts

Vest

Running spikes

Socks

Good for :
Speed
Strength
Endurance
Mental toughness
Agility

Gymnastics

... in 30 seconds

The Ancient Greeks believed that health and fitness were important for all. Men exercised naked, in an open space called a gymnasium – the origin of the word 'gymnastics'.

Olga Korbut

Men's gymnastics was part of the first modern Olympic Games in 1896, but women's gymnastics wasn't an Olympic sport until 1936. The six men's events focus mainly on strength and flexibility, while the four events for women highlight acrobatic skills and technique.

International contests are organized by the International Federation of Gymnastics, and there are regular World Championship events for each discipline. Gymnasts train hard, often practicing above a foam-filled pit to avoid injury. In a competition, they are awarded up to 10 points by a team of judges for their performances. A winner is declared in each event, and the gymnast with the highest total score wins overall.

Kohei Uchimura from Japan is famous for his extremely difficult routines. He has won 19 World Championship medals as well as gold and silver at the Olympics. In 1972, aged just 17, Russian gymnast Olga Korbut's acrobatics and technique – including a backwards flip on the balance beam – helped make gymnastics a globally popular sport.

3-second sum-up

Gymnastics combines strength, flexibility and acrobatics.

3-minute mission Balance challenge

You need: A clear space • A timer • A friend

1. Stand on one leg and stretch your arms out to the sides while your friend times how long you can balance.

2. Now close both eyes and try again. Compare the times.

Our eyes help us to make minor movements to stay balanced. This is why balancing with closed eyes is a lot harder than with them open.

Gymnasts need to combine acrobatic skills and graceful moves with flexibility and body strength. There are different disciplines for men and women.

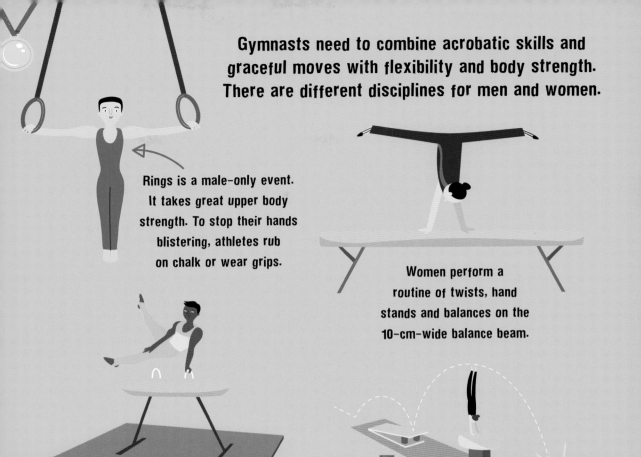

Rings is a male-only event. It takes great upper body strength. To stop their hands blistering, athletes rub on chalk or wear grips.

Women perform a routine of twists, hand stands and balances on the 10-cm-wide balance beam.

During a pommel horse routine, the gymnast keeps his feet pointed and legs straight.

In a vault, the gymnast leaps from a springboard to land hands first on the apparatus.

Leotard

Leggings

Pumps

Vest

Gymnastic clothing is designed for maximum comfort and freedom of movement.

Good for :
Balance
Flexibility
Upper-body strength
Lower-body strength
Agility

Cycling

... in 30 seconds

This two-wheeled sport followed the invention of the bicycle in Germany, in about 1817. The first recorded bike race happened in Paris, France, in 1878. The competitors raced 1,200 metres on solid rubber tyres – ouch!

Cycling today is a popular sport that is open to everyone. There is a wide choice of events: road racing, track racing, mountain biking, BMX, cycle cross and cycle speedway. Each kind of event takes place on a different terrain, requires a specific type of cycle and makes different demands on the rider.

Chris Froome

Track and road cycling, BMX and mountain biking are all Olympic sports. For maximum success in these events, the cyclists' fitness and skills are combined with the latest technology in materials and equipment. Cyclists and scientists often work in a wind tunnel to find the fastest cycling positions, test new types of bike frame, or assess the safest, most aerodynamic helmet.

British road racer, Chris Froome, is one of the most successful cyclists ever. In 2017, he won the famous Tour de France race for the fourth time. Another top cyclist, Laura Kenny, has 12 World Championship and four Olympic gold medals. She is the most successful female track cyclist in Olympic history.

3-second sum-up

There are six different cycle sports. New technology is helping cyclists set new records.

The Yellow Jersey

Cyclists in the Tour de France road race compete in four categories. The top riders at the end of each stage are awarded a coloured jersey to wear:

YELLOW – worn by the overall leader.

GREEN – awarded to the best sprinter.

RED SPOTTED – goes to the best mountain climber.

WHITE – the prize for the fastest rider aged under 25.

Cycling sports take place on different terrains using different styles of cycle.

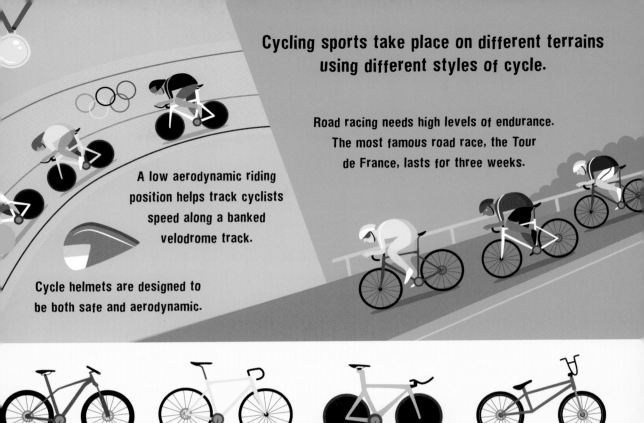

Road racing needs high levels of endurance. The most famous road race, the Tour de France, lasts for three weeks.

A low aerodynamic riding position helps track cyclists speed along a banked velodrome track.

Cycle helmets are designed to be both safe and aerodynamic.

Mountain   **Road**   **Track**   **BMX**

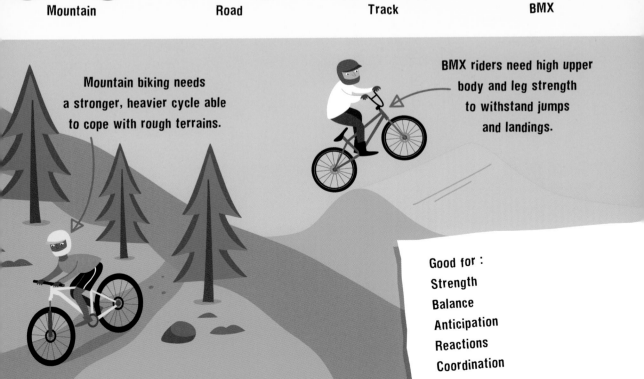

Mountain biking needs a stronger, heavier cycle able to cope with rough terrains.

BMX riders need high upper body and leg strength to withstand jumps and landings.

Good for :
Strength
Balance
Anticipation
Reactions
Coordination

Motor sports

... in 30 seconds

The sport of motor racing began at the end of the 1800s, soon after the car was invented. Most early races tested reliability more than speed. The first cars built for racing appeared in the 1920s and '30s. Today, a variety of race cars compete in a range of events.

Single-seater racing is exciting and dangerous. The wheels are outside the car body, the driver sits in an open cockpit and the circuit is engineered for speed. The top races – Formula 1 and IndyCar – attract thousands of spectators worldwide. Younger drivers can try kart racing – a fun, safer form of single-seater circuit racing.

Danica
Patrick

Sports cars are built for high speed but have a closed cockpit and wheels. The annual Le Mans 24-hour race is an endurance test for the cars and drivers. It starts and finishes in the mid-afternoon, so three drivers take turns to race day and night. Adapted road cars take part in touring car racing and in rallying, where they race on closed roads or off-road along tracks.

Brazilian Formula 1 driver, Ayrton Senna, won the world title three times. He was said to be one of the greatest the sport has ever seen. The American Danica Patrick is thought of as a role model for women in a traditionally male sport. She was the first female to win an IndyCar Series race.

3-second sum-up

The different kinds of motor sports use specially built or modified cars.

3-minute mission Reaction test

Racing drivers need to react quickly. Try this experiment.

You need: A plastic ruler • A friend

1. Hold the ruler vertically between your finger and thumb at arm's length. Get your friend to place their open finger and thumb around the end of the ruler, ready to catch it.

2. Drop the ruler. Note the measure on the ruler where it was caught. Swap places and repeat the test.

In motor sports, different types of vehicles compete in races that test endurance as well as speed.

Rallycross vehicles have been adapted to race off-road.

In the world-famous Le Mans sports car race, competitors drive day and night for 24 hours.

Kart racing is a scaled-down version of circuit racing, and open to everyone.

Formula 1 is the fastest form of single-seater racing. The driver sits in an open cockpit and cars race wheel to wheel.

Touring car vehicles are converted road cars with a closed cockpit and covered wheels.

A more advanced Formula 1 sports car is designed every year. The race car engineers tap into the latest technology to source better, lighter materials and CAD (computer-aided design) programs are used to plot the aerodynamics of the overall shape.

Good for :
Reactions
Neck strength
Shoulder strength
Concentration
Core stability

Combat sports

... in 30 seconds

Many ancient Olympic sports, such as wrestling, were based on fighting. Violence was common and Roman gladiators – 'swordsmen' in Latin – often fought to the death in public contests. These days combat sports follow strict safety rules and focus on respect for an opponent.

Sports including wrestling, judo, fencing, boxing and taekwondo are part of the modern Olympic Games. The rules are different for each event, but the winner is usually the contestant who gains the most points. Since safety is always the top priority, a referee watches the action closely to make sure the rules are followed.

Muhammad Ali

Most combat sports take place in a ring or on a large mat. Fighters may wear mouthguards and other compulsory protective clothing, such as headgear. Combat sports are popular across the world, and both men and women are encouraged to take part.

The American heavyweight boxer Muhammad Ali was World Heavyweight Champion three times. He's regarded as one of the best boxers and most influential people of recent times. The judo fighter, Majlinda Kelmendi, won gold at the 2016 Olympics – the first athlete from newly independent Kosovo to win a medal.

3-second sum-up

Modern combat sports are governed by strict safety rules.

Marathon match

The longest ever boxing match was in 1893, in New Orleans, USA. The fight between Andy Bowen and Jack Burke went on for 7 hours and 19 minutes – or 111 three-minute rounds! – before it was stopped. The referee, who was probably pretty tired too, felt that the men were too dazed to continue, so he declared the fight a draw.

There are three types of combat sports – hitting, weaponry and grappling.

Taekwondo uses fast high, jump and spin kicks.

Competitors wear a white uniform and protective equipment.

Helmet

Body shield

Groin shield

Gloves

Shin guards

Fencing is based on traditional swordsmanship. Points are won by making contact.

Fencers have puncture-resistant clothing and equipment.

Jacket

Breeches

Mask

Foil

Plastron

Gloves

In a judo contest the aim is to throw or pin the opponent onto their back, using the correct technique to score an ippon – winning point.

Contestants wear a loose-fitting white or blue uniform tied with a coloured belt.

Good for :
Reactions
Coordination
Strength
Balance
Flexiblity

Tennis

... in 30 seconds

A 12th-century game, a bit like handball, was the ancestor of modern tennis. A racquet was used to hit the ball and the game was popular at the French royal court. 'Real' or 'royal' tennis is still played today.

Martina
Navratilova

The modern sport came about because of a garden tool! In 1830, a mechanical mower was used to cut a grass pitch, and lawn tennis was born. Modern tennis matches are either 'singles' (between two players) or 'doubles' (between two pairs of players). As well as playing on grass, the game is also played on a clay court, or indoors on a rubber surface.

Players compete in several games to win a match. The first to reach four points wins the game – if they are two points ahead. The first to win six games wins the set – if they are two games ahead. If the score is six games each, a tie-break is played and the set goes to whoever reaches seven points with a two-point lead. The first player to gain two sets in a three-set match, or three sets in a five-set match wins overall.

Martina Navratilova played for the USA and won a record-breaking 168 singles titles and 79 doubles titles in her awesome 30-year career. Swiss player, Roger Federer, is seen as the best male player of all time. He has won more Grand Slam singles titles than any other man.

3-second sum-up

Tennis developed from a medieval game and a lawnmower into an international sport.

Scoring

Tennis has an unusual scoring system, which comes from the historic French game.

Love = zero points	15 = 1 point
30 = 2 points	40 = 3 points
Game = 4 points	Deuce = 4 points each

'Love' comes from *l'oeuf*, the French for 'an egg' – the same shape as a zero.

Tennis players compete against each other in two-player singles matches and four-player doubles matches on indoor and outdoor courts.

A player making a forehand stroke swings their entire arm back, around and up to hit the ball in the centre of the racquet.

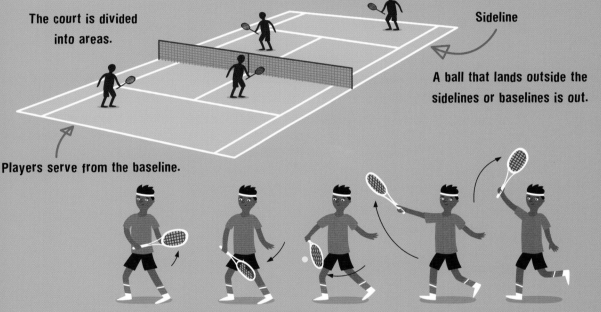

The court is divided into areas.

Sideline

A ball that lands outside the sidelines or baselines is out.

Players serve from the baseline.

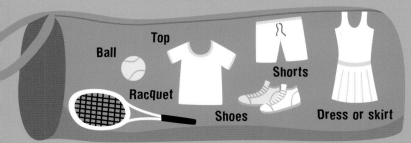

It is harder to make a precise backhand stroke. A firm grip on the racquet, good footwork and a powerful up stroke are essential.

Ball

Top

Racquet

Shoes

Shorts

Dress or skirt

Good for :
Coordination
Upper body strength
Flexibility
Agility

Golf

... in 30 seconds

The modern sport of golf has its roots in a 600-year-old game from Scotland, in which a small rock was hit around sand dunes and tracks with a stick. Today golf is a popular sport all over the world.

The game is usually played on a large course dotted with 18 numbered holes. Players use a set of curved clubs to hit the ball around the course and into each hole. The course features different types of ground, from smooth fairways, unmowed areas called roughs and deep sandpit-like bunkers, to the circular 'green' around the 10.7cm-wide hole.

Arnold
Palmer

The distance and hazards, such as bunkers, from the tee (starting point) to the green vary, so each hole has a score called a 'par'. The par is the ideal number of shots a player should take to get the ball into the hole. After completing a round of 18 holes, the golfer with the lowest total number of strokes is the winner.

Men's and women's golf has a total of nine top-level annual tournaments, called the 'Majors'. Famous American player, Arnold Palmer, won six Majors in his long career. Annika Sorenstam, from Sweden, is one of the best-ever female golfers. She won over 90 tournaments, including four Majors.

3-second sum-up

Golfers use different clubs to send a ball around a course and into 18 holes in the fewest hits.

3-minute mission Dominant eye

In many sports it helps to keep one eye on the ball. Try this test to find out which is your dominant eye.

With the back of your hands facing you, place your thumbs at right angles, one above the other. Then move the fingers of one hand over the other, to form a small triangle.

Look at an object through the triangle. Centre the object in the triangle and close one eye. If the object disappears, use the other eye to look. When you can still see the object you've found your dominant eye!

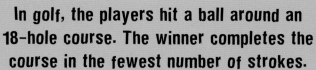

In golf, the players hit a ball around an 18-hole course. The winner completes the course in the fewest number of strokes.

Areas of rough and smooth ground affect the kind of shot the player makes. Hitting the ball a long way requires a powerful driving shot.

If the ball ends up in rough grass or a sand trap, the player uses a short, upward chip shot to hit it out.

Different clubs are used. Heavy 'woods' are for long-distance shots, angled 'irons' for short or tricky shots, and light putters for tapping the ball into the hole.

Hitting the ball into a hole without making too many strokes takes an accurate putting shot.

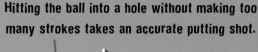

Good for :
Coordination
Flexibility
Core stability
Upper-body strength
Mental toughness
Balance

Discover more

NON-FICTION BOOKS

Children's Book of Sport
by DK Childrens, 2011

i-spy Sports and Games by DK
Michelin Guides, 2010

The Paralympics by Nick Hunter
Wayland, 2012

The Sports Book
DK, 2016

The Story of the Olympics
by Richard Brassey
Orion, 2016

The Top Ten of Everything in Sports
by Editors of Sports Illustrated Kids
Liberty Street, 2017

*The What on Earth? Wallbook of
Sport* by Brian Oliver, Christopher
Lloyd and Andy Forshaw
What on Earth Publishing, 2012

BOOKS ABOUT SPORTSPEOPLE

Ultimate Sports Heroes series
Dino Books, 2017

*Women in Sport: Fifty Fearless
Athletes Who Played to Win*
by Rachel Ignotofsky
Wren & Rook, 2018

E BOOKS

*Spectator Guides: Aquatics,
Gymnastics, Track & Field, Cycling*
by Usborne Media, 2016
Kindle

WEBSITES

BBC Bitesize *https://www.bbc.co.uk/education/subjects/zj6pyrd*

CBBC *https://www.bbc.co.uk/cbbc/topics/sport*

International Olympic Committee *https://www.olympic.org/the-ioc*

and *https://www.olympic.org/videos*

International Paralympic Committee *https://www.paralympic.org*

Learn4Good.com: Online sports games *https://www.learn4good.com/kids-games/sports.htm*

Sports Illustrated Kids magazine *https://www.sikids.com*

Sports science activities *http://www.sciencekids.co.nz/sports.html*

Although every endeavour has been made by the publisher to ensure that all content from these websites is educational material of the highest quality and is age appropriate, we strongly advise that Internet access is supervised by a responsible adult.

Index

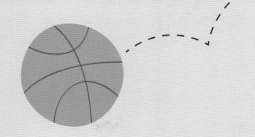

Index

Answers
Page 44: Olympic Events quiz
The following were NOT events
in the early modern Olympics:
Hopping
One-legged balance
Poodle clipping